THE DILEMMA OF THE
ALCOHOLIC MARRIAGE

"Marriage is that relation between men and women in which the independence is equal, the dependence mutual and the obligation reciprocal."

—L. Anspacher

The Al-Anon Family Groups are a fellowship of relatives and friends of alcoholics who share their experience, strength, and hope in order to solve their common problems. We believe alcoholism is a family illness and that changed attitudes can aid recovery.

Al-Anon is not allied with any sect, denomination, political entity, organization, or institution; does not engage in any controversy; neither endorses nor opposes any cause. There are no dues for membership. Al-Anon is self-supporting through its own voluntary contributions.

Al-Anon has but one purpose: to help families of alcoholics. We do this by practicing the Twelve Steps, by welcoming and giving comfort to families of alcoholics, and by giving understanding and encouragement to the alcoholic.

Suggested Preamble to the Twelve Steps

Al-Anon books that may be helpful:

Alateen—Hope for Children of Alcoholics (B-3)

The Dilemma of the Alcoholic Marriage (B-4)

The Al-Anon Family Groups—Classic Edition (B-5)

One Day at a Time in Al-Anon (B-6), Large Print (B-14)

Lois Remembers (B-7)

Al-Anon's Twelve Steps & Twelve Traditions (B-8)

Alateen—a day at a time (B-10)

As We Understood . . . (B-11)

. . . In All Our Affairs: Making Crises Work for You (B-15)

Courage to Change—One Day at a Time in Al-Anon II (B-16), Large Print (B-17)

From Survival to Recovery: Growing Up in an Alcoholic Home (B-21)

How Al-Anon Works for Families & Friends of Alcoholics (B-22)

Courage to Be Me—Living with Alcoholism (B-23)

Paths to Recovery—Al-Anon's Steps, Traditions, and Concepts (B-24)

Living Today in Alateen (B-26)

Hope for Today (B-27), Large Print (B-28)

Opening Our Hearts, Transforming Our Losses (B-29)

Discovering Choices (B-30)

THE DILEMMA

OF THE

ALCOHOLIC MARRIAGE

Al-Anon Family Group Headquarters, Inc.
World Service Office for Al-Anon and Alateen

For information and catalog of literature write to
World Service Office for Al-Anon and Alateen:

Al-Anon Family Group Headquarters, Inc.
1600 Corporate Landing Parkway
Virginia Beach, VA 23454-5617
757-563-1600   Fax 757-563-1656
E-mail: wso@al-anon.org
Web site: al-anon.org/members

This book is also available in: Dutch, Finnish, French, German, Icelandic, Italian, Japanese, Polish, Portuguese, Russian, and Spanish.

Al-Anon/Alateen is supported by members' voluntary contributions and from the sale of our Conference Approved Literature.

Library of Congress Catalog Card No. 70-182-133
ISBN 978-0-910034-18-0

Publisher's Cataloging in Publication
The dilemma of the alcoholic marriage/Al-Anon Family Groups, Inc.
p. cm.
Reissue of work first published in 1971.
Includes index.

1. Alcoholics—Family relationships. 2. Alcoholism—Psychological aspects. 3. Alcoholism—Treatment. 4. Alcoholism. I. Al-Anon Family Group Headquarters, inc.
HV5132.D5 1992   362.29'2'3
                                                    QB192-1524

 Approved by
World Service Conference
Al-Anon Family Groups

CONTENTS

HOW TO
FIND HELP

If you have a problem involving alcoholism, whether in a spouse, a son or daughter, a parent or a friend, you will find Al-Anon Family Groups a dependable source of help.

You can get information about meetings by telephoning any number listed under Al-Anon in your telephone book, or under the local number of Alcoholics Anonymous (A.A.), or by contacting the World Service Office for Al-Anon and Alateen:

Al-Anon Family Group Headquarters, Inc.
1600 Corporate Landing Parkway
Virginia Beach, VA. 23454-5617
757-563-1600   Fax 757-563-1655
E-mail: wso@al-anon.org

A catalog of available literature-inexpensive leaflets, books and booklets will be sent to you on request. Our monthly magazine, *The Forum*, is available by paid subscription.

INTRODUCTION:
HOW AL-ANON WORKS

The Al-Anon program is essentially a personal re-orientation process based on the Twelve Steps of Alcoholics Anonymous (A.A.).

The Al-Anon Family Groups make up a fellowship of men and women whose lives have been disturbed by another's compulsive drinking. The members share their experience, strength, and hope with each other in a continuing effort to achieve serenity.

The groups meet to discuss the problems created by alcoholism. It is an informal fellowship whose members try to uncover and discourage their own negative reactions, while building on their positive qualities. The meetings provide an atmosphere in which the members learn to recognize their own faulty attitudes which may be aggravating the family difficulties.

Al-Anon offers its members a supportive group in which they can find peace of mind and build self-confidence.

The wives and husbands of compulsive drinkers often find it difficult to adjust to the personal characteristics, traits, and attitudes of the alcoholic, whether sober or still drinking.

This is especially true in the more intimate areas of the marriage relationship, personal communication, and sex.

The World Service Office (WSO) of the Al-Anon Family Groups receives hundreds of letters each year from troubled and bewildered people in all parts of the world. They want to know how to deal with the maladjustments in their marriages, difficulties which often were realized only after the alcoholic had settled into sobriety.

While the active drinking was still the major problem, the spouse wished only that the alcoholic might become sober. That was to be the magic solution to all problems. But sobriety alone often fails to bring about the hoped-for improvement.

The problems which beset the families of alcoholics who are still drinking often bring the spouses to Al-Anon in search of solutions. The difficulties which disrupt family life are physical and verbal violence, disturbed children, peril to health and safety, unpaid bills, and often actual deprivation of such necessities as food and clothing.

With such problems Al-Anon has a long record of success. It can and does help those who really want help. Its group work consists of a sharing of experience, strength, and hope; the program guides its members to a better understanding and more willing acceptance of themselves. Al-Anon gives them a fresh point of view from which to approach their difficulties.

The Al-Anon program works. This is proved by the many thousands who have found in it the way to more constructive attitudes toward themselves and their families. They learn to overcome such negative emotions as resentment and self-pity. The resulting change often motivates the alcoholic to seek help.

*   *   *

For the sake of simplicity, the spouse of an alcoholic will be referred to as the wife except in the chapter for men. It is understood that most of the material applies to the husband of an alcoholic as well.

AL-ANON IS FOR GUIDANCE—
NOT FOR COUNSELING

The basic purpose of Al-Anon is to help us, its members, solve our personal problems. It is important for the newcomer to realize that our fellow members are not equipped, by training or experience, to advise, judge or counsel in intimate personal problems, and particularly not in those involving complex family relationships. That is the function of the psychiatrist, the clergyman, the social worker, or others with a professional background for this work.

There has been a great deal of research by professionals into the effects of alcoholism on marriage. The results of this research are usually of interest only to other professionals in this field because they are written in language too technical for the average reader. And those which are written for the general public rarely make suggestions that an individual could successfully apply to his or her problem. Those who work in the field of marital relations know it is futile and sometimes even dangerous to make recommendations without personal consultation with the people involved. Each situation is unique; each is confused by conflicting emotions and reactions that are rarely the same in any two cases.

The members of Al-Anon are cautioned not to give advice about what course of action is right for another person to take, even if the advice is asked for. Our program is based on the conviction that most of us have the power to bring about substantial changes in our relationships and living conditions, by searching out and correcting our own shortcomings. As such changes occur, each of us will know what course of action is right for the particular time and situation.

The Spouse as an Individual

Al-Anon encourages us to become aware of ourselves as individuals and of others as well.

Increased awareness of themselves and each other, which both partners can gain through understanding and practice of the A.A. and Al-Anon programs, can solve many seemingly insoluble problems. This has been the experience of many thousands of members.

The open door to helpful answers is communication based on love. Such communication depends on awareness of and respect for each other's unique individuality. This also means concern for each other's well-being and willingness to accept in another what may not measure up to our own standards and expectations. Such love also requires a measure of self-esteem, an awareness of our own good qualities. The Commandment "Thou shalt love thy neighbor as thyself," clearly implies that we cannot love others unless we feel ourselves worthy of being loved. Thus Al-Anon also teaches us the unique value of our own persons and lives. Just as no other human being should be subject to our control, so we, too, must feel free to reject tyrannical domination. For all of us are, in the last analysis, subject only to whatever Higher Power we choose as a guide for our lives.

The poet Rainer Maria Rilke said it this way:

"Once we realize that even between the closest human beings infinite distances continue to exist, a wonderful living side by side can grow up if they succeed in loving the distance between them, which

3

makes it possible for each to see the other whole against the sky. A good marriage is that in which each appoints the other guardian of his individuality."

Each of us is responsible to himself and for himself. As the cofounder of Al-Anon has said, "We can't get into someone else's head and turn the wheels that will make him behave in the way we think is right."

Applied to the close personal relationship of marriage, this gives each partner freedom to be himself, to strive for a good adjustment to life in his or her own way. And far from creating an impersonal relationship, this emphasis on one's own individuality creates mutual respect and trust which are the very foundations of a good marriage.

THE NATURE OF
THE DILEMMA

While the drinking is active, and day-to-day problems absorb the attention and energies of the spouse of an alcoholic, the matter of sexual maladjustment often falls into the background. There may be difficulties, of course. Some alcoholics, sexually stimulated by liquor, may make brutally aggressive and sometimes violent assaults, to which their spouses react with fear or disgust. Others become totally incompetent sexually, depriving their partners of this vital element of marriage.

The interaction and attitudes established in such ways are often too deep to be changed simply by the alcoholic becoming sober. Years of compulsive drinking may have brought about radical emotional changes in both partners to the marriage: the alcoholic may be inhibited by guilt over his behavior while he was drinking, the spouse by remembered violence, deprivations, infidelities, and other humiliations. These reactions may persist even long after the drinker has become sober. Help is needed to reestablish a healthier relationship.

Troubled wives and husbands often take it for granted that their marital discords are due entirely to alcoholism, whether the alcoholic is sober or is still drinking. Yet alcoholism itself rarely creates all these problems, and sobriety itself usually does not cure them.

Many professionals in the fields of human relations believe that alcoholism and sexual maladjustment have a common psychological basis. The alcoholic may, for reasons deeply buried in the subconscious, find sexual adjustment difficult.

When a woman marries a man who drinks alcoholically, she may be accepting a sex problem along with the alcoholism. Many a person enters blithely into such a marriage with the romantic notion that love will overcome all—that the magic of togetherness will transform the devoted but alcoholic lover into a sober, responsible husband. This risk is often doomed to failure. She soon learns that even love is no match for the compelling desire for alcohol.

And to make matters worse, she may find herself confronted with a sexual inadequacy or indifference that in itself may stand in the way of his achieving sobriety.

On the other hand, a woman who is maladjusted sexually herself, due to influences in her background, may find a convenient excuse for her problem by blaming it on the alcoholic.

A man who marries an alcoholic may find he has a wonderful sex partner as long as she is drinking, but that she becomes unresponsive when sober. Or if he is unable to respond to her sexual demands because he finds her unattractive, even repulsive when she is drunk, she may humiliate and ridicule him. Such scenes are not easily forgotten and can cause difficulties which carry over into sobriety.

Yet one dependable fact emerges: the reestablishment of a satisfactory sex relationship may be brought about if both partners are willing to contribute to the partnership the patience, loyalty, respect and honesty which are built into the Al-Anon program.

With this in mind, we have ventured to deal with this broad and tangled subject because we believe that the principles by which Al-Anon members try to live can help to solve this problem, as it does so many others.

An earnest and concentrated study of the Al-Anon program, in depth, will help us to become more tolerant, confident, and loving, teaching us to accept the faults of others as we seek to correct shortcomings in ourselves.

The Alcoholic's Dual Personality

The changes that alcohol creates in a person are difficult to understand and still more difficult to cope with. The alcoholic's hidden guilt and unhappiness may reveal themselves in torrents of explosive temper and accusations, to which the spouse impulsively reacts by feeling hurt, until she learns in Al-Anon that it is futile to take these outbursts seriously. She thinks he really means what he is saying, which compels her to defend herself against his unjust attacks by fighting back. She doesn't realize that his rage is really at himself and that he must vent it on the nearest person. He knows from experience that he will get the reaction he wants, which helps to ease his guilt feelings.

It is at such times that the spouse may decide in

desperation that something must be done, that she must take steps to free herself from this intolerable situation. But if the alcoholic's mood has a change for the better, she may forget her resolve and hope that somehow things will get better.

This is especially true if the violent episode is followed by a spell of sobriety and the alcoholic reverts temporarily to his old self. Then hope is reborn and the wife's "decision" vanishes from her mind. She once more sees him as he is, the man she married. She doesn't allow herself to face the fact that what has happened so often will certainly happen again as long as he continues to drink, and she continues to react in the same way to his irrational behavior. When she comes to the point of recognizing the dual personality of the alcoholic as a whole, she will know how to change her own attitudes and course of action.

She may, too, in the times of sobriety, be tempted to admit to a fault or otherwise expose a sensitive side of her nature only to find that when he drinks again he will use her confidences to hurt her through ridicule or accusation. When this happens repeatedly, she becomes wary and is careful to guard against sharing confidences with him.

To see this situation realistically, she would have to understand how desperately the guilt-tormented alcoholic needs such weapons to bolster his own ego. When he uses these weapons to attack, it is not because he hates his wife but because he hates himself and needs to reassure himself that he is not all bad. He finds fault with the person nearest to him because it makes it a little easier for him to tolerate himself.

The spouse, seeing it only as a betrayal of her trusts, withdraws more and more, keeping their conversations less and less intimate. Such fear of being hurt can cause severe breakdowns in communication.

WHAT MANNER OF COMMUNICATIONS ARE THESE?

The quality of human relationships depends largely upon the way we communicate with each other. It depends not only on what we say, but how we say it; not only on what we do, but our motives for doing it. Our tone of voice and even our smallest actions are elements of communication; many of us are hardly aware of these.

When partners in a marriage are held together by a bond of love, mutual respect, and a desire to please and comfort, communication naturally falls into patterns that express these feelings and give both husband and wife confidence in each other and a sense of security and mutual dependence.

When a relationship is distorted by an unbalanced dependence, or by suspicion, hostility, excessive demands, and expectations, these flaws reveal themselves in the way the two people communicate with each other.

If a man marries a woman because he was attracted by her warm maternal quality, as many alcoholics do, he is likely to be the dependent one. And she, attracted to him because of her unconscious desire to mother someone, will be the practical member of the family. She may later bemoan the fact that he has failed in his role as head of the house, not aware that it was she who took the reins and did all the managing. And while she is managing him, the children, the household, and the finances, she's awash with self-pity because of the big load she has to carry.

If he is drinking, her constant protective watchfulness makes it easy for him to sidestep getting help. He has no incentive to get sober. She convinces herself that she's doing her very best for him; she hasn't learned, as she would in Al-Anon, that shielding him from the consequences of his drinking only prolongs its course.

When he's drunk, her reaction is to reproach him for his behavior, and that's the very worst time to attempt to communicate with him. In fact it can't be done without triggering a family war.

Until she learns what is wrong with *her* attitude and how to change *herself* so he will be forced to face his responsibilities, the situation isn't likely to improve.

If a man married a woman because she's shy, timid and submissive, he unconsciously chose a wife who would satisfy his need to dominate. If she turns out to be an alcoholic, he will have the complete dependent he wants, no matter how desperately he *thinks* he wants her sober. He, too, will cover up her drinking, protect her from public disgrace, and assume all the responsibilities which should be hers.

Such distorted relationships are often found in alcoholic marriages, and they inevitably lead to the drying up of the communication which is vital to a good marriage.

We can make verbal communication effective if we never lose sight of the fact that the alcoholic is sick; he has a disease for which it is unfair to blame him or punish him. But he must be told—at the right time and without anger or reproach—what he has done and is doing.

This suggestion, from an A.A. member, has proved successful in many cases.

"The alcoholic may experience blackouts. He

appears to be functioning, but he usually doesn't remember what he did or said. He suspects that something did happen and his anxiety and nameless guilt are almost unbearable. If you're sorry for him, you might think it's unfair to torture him by telling him *what* his drinking led to. But it's kinder and more constructive to relieve his mind and tell him frankly what he needs to know. He has a right to know what his drinking is doing to him. If you go to him without anger or reproach and tell him quietly what happened, you'll be helping him to see himself as he is.

"My wife did just this for me and it was the single most helpful thing that ever happened to bring me to sobriety.

"I had no idea how far I had fallen from my own ideals until she came to me one morning and told me what I had done the night before. And as soon as she had spoken her piece, she excused herself and quietly left me to figure out for myself what I was going to do about it.

"But the alcoholic must be allowed to draw his own conclusions. If you tell him *how* he looked, *how* he acted, what you think of him for it, it won't work. He'll just fall back on the old excuse, 'She's picking on me again,' and he'll have a grievance against you that will sustain him over this bad time."

Until the spouse has been exposed to the Al-Anon program, she automatically assumes that the alcoholic could, if he only wanted to, get sober and behave better, so she berates him when he comes home drunk. And when the drunk phase is past, she hesitates to bring up even urgent problems for fear of giving him reason for another binge.

This brings to mind a meeting that inspired the members to explore their own motives and to understand how they were performing in their communication with their partners. The topic was:

Do You Say What You Mean?
Do You Mean What You Say?

Many of the difficulties of achieving good communication lie not only with the alcoholic, but with the spouse as well. The stresses and uncertainties she lives with each day—the dread, the fear, the anger—have so distorted her reasoning powers that most of her reactions are emotional and often destructive.

The chairman asked the members, "Why don't we say what we mean? Why aren't we honest enough to confront the troublesome partner with some straight truths? They're surely obvious enough, but if we fail to let the alcoholic know how we feel about things, how will he know? What's going to motivate him to find sobriety if we let him believe that his behavior is acceptable?"

Each person spoke in turn; these were the answers.

"I don't say what I think because I want to avoid fights and trouble. I guess I haven't learned to distinguish between saying disagreeable, critical things and making plain statements about a situation that will throw light on them without hurting his feelings."

The next speaker said,

"I'm afraid to tell him what I think. Usually I think of nothing but criticizing him for what he's doing, and I know that's wrong because he's sick. And when he's sober he's so nice and kind that I hate to bring up the unpleasant things that happened. And anyway aren't we supposed to work on ourselves in this program? Telling him how we feel about the things he does seems to me the same as taking his inventory."

Commenting on these two remarks, the chairman said,

"You know that no improvement can be accomplished unless we're consistent. If we haven't the courage to speak up when the drinker is in a sober phase, he'll just go on believing that there's no limit to what we'll tolerate. But we have to know what we think before we can say it convincingly. We can't just bury it and hide our heads under a blanket of hope. Our husbands have a right to know what we expect from them. It's up to them to decide whether or not they want to live up to our expectations. Not letting them know how we feel is dishonest. It's just another way of pretending we accept the situation when we don't. It's a cop-out. If we want the alcoholic to face reality, we must face it first, and not be afraid to share our feelings. I don't think that's the same as nagging as long as we don't repeat ourselves, and I don't think it's the same as taking his inventory. What do you think?"

The next member spoke up, "It's bad enough to sidestep saying what we mean, but it's even worse to say what we don't mean. My long-standing habit of 'blowing my top' when my husband was drinking lasted long after he was sober in A.A.. I reacted to anything that annoyed me with the first angry words that came to my mind. I'd forget that he was just getting back some of his long-lost self-esteem, and would say something bitter that would undermine it. I guess I wanted to hurt him because of all he'd put me through in the past. But I'm getting over that. I began to realize that the hurtful things I was saying really hit home—he actually believed them and I didn't mean them at all! I'm doing better as time goes on, but I have to keep reminding myself, 'Don't say it unless you mean it,' and that has kept me from saying a lot of things I'd later wish I hadn't."

What emerged out of that meeting was finally summed up by the chairman.

"We can say what we mean only if we have the courage to be honest, with ourselves and with others. We must know why we are saying it. If it's to impress, to belittle, to convey our self-pity and resentment, it ought not be said. That would only widen the rift and we want to close that gap! And we can mean what we say only if we stop the rash statements before they hit the air.

"Now let's all go home and try to do a better job of saying what we really mean, and not saying what we don't mean."

What Do Your Actions Communicate?

Telling the alcoholic what we expect and how we feel may have gotten us nowhere. He may just ignore us as if we hadn't said anything. More talking would just be nagging. So sometimes, we think some kind of action is necessary.

This, too, is a form of communication. It says, "I respect your right to live the way you want to. But I also have that right. I will not let your drinking be the most important thing in my life."

This typical discussion at an Al-Anon meeting suggests approaches to such a difficulty.

"When my husband stops at a bar on his way home from work every night, there's no telling when he will turn up. If I have dinner at a regular hour with the children, he may come just as we're finishing. Then he's highly indignant because we didn't wait. I've tried fixing his plate and keeping it warm, but by ten or eleven it's dried up and he's just as likely to hurl plate and all at me. I know I can't reach him with reasoning, so what do I do?"

One member answered,

"Tell him, on an occasion when he's sober, that you want the children to have their meals at a regular hour, and that you want yours too, so you'll have dinner at six whether he's home or not."

Another member said,

"Why say anything? Actions speak louder than words. If six o'clock leaves him ample time to get home from work, set your dinner hour for six and eat then, whether he's there or not."

A third member spoke up,

"I disagree. It's true that 'Actions speak louder than words.' But if you don't say anything to him when he's sober, he won't know what to expect. You'll just have a scene the next time he's late, and it's impossible to reason with him when he's been drinking. You might explain to him that you haven't made this decision because you don't want him to eat with the family. That would be punishing him. It's just that you think the children would do better on a regular schedule. That's keeping the family from revolving around his drinking."

A husband spoke up,

"After working hard all day, I would come home and find my wife too drunk to prepare dinner for my children and me. During a period when my wife wasn't drinking, I sat down and talked with her as calmly and reasonably as I could. I told her that she was the only one who could do anything about her drinking, but that I could take certain steps to see that her drinking would not affect me and our children as far as meals were concerned. I arranged with a neighbor to come in and cook the dinner. This went on for three weeks, then my wife asked for another chance. Although she still gets drunk nearly every night, now she at least waits until after she has cooked dinner. I think this is a case of 'changing the things we can.'"

These suggestions have certain qualities in common: they are honest and candid, they are courageous and firm, they have no element of blame or criticism and they are courteous.

A very large order, but communication which has these qualities will accomplish several ends: It will confirm our individuality and dignity; the person who hears them cannot mistake their meaning; they carry no residue of regret for unfairness.

Coping with Anger

What alcoholism is doing to us gives rise to resentment. Resentment creates anger, and our anger must be dealt with, for our own health and growth.

Living with an alcoholic can be a frustrating business, producing conflict after conflict. Even after the spouse has begun to absorb and use the principles of Al-Anon and has learned not to make a bad situation worse by arguing, the alcoholic's behavior will often make her seethe with anger.

Both before and after sobriety is established, the alcoholic may say and do things that trouble her. The resentment may take the form of inner, unexpressed anger, or in those of us who are more volatile and high-strung, recurrent senseless rages. If this self-destructive behavior is allowed to continue, no real growth, spiritual or emotional, can be expected.

As we gain a deeper understanding of ourselves in the Al-Anon program, we learn more wholesome ways to relieve our feelings of hostility by analyzing and uncovering their causes. Otherwise they can have two undesirable consequences:

1) We suppress the anger, turning it back into ourselves to fester, which can make us sick, mentally and physically.

2) We "take out" our feelings on others, particularly our children, whose healthy development can be seriously hampered by an unreasonable and hostile parent.

One member illustrated this at an Al-Anon meeting:

"When I first came into Al-Anon, a battered and defeated victim of many a brawl with my husband when he was drinking, I heard one phrase and latched onto it.

"'Keep your mouth shut, no matter what he says!'

"I thought that was all the magic I needed, so I immediately began to exercise massive self-control when he was drinking. I thought I was the picture of serenity. But it seemed to make him all the more furious; he wanted me to help create a full-fledged fight as usual.

"The worst, though, was what it did to me. It made me so frustrated, so nervous, that I began to take it out on my children. The least thing they did that bothered me, like a bit of spilled milk or childish wrangling, would cause me to fly into an uncontrollable rage until I had exhausted myself and sat trembling with fear at what my terrible temper was doing to my little ones. I realized that I was punishing them for what had been done to me. I knew I would have to find other outlets for these feelings.

"Soon afterward it was my good fortune, or maybe that's the way things happen in Al-Anon, to hear a speaker from another group tell a story very much like mine. She told us what she did about her anger instead of repressing it or venting it on innocent victims. Here's her story just as she wrote it out for me afterward to help me solve my problem.

"'When my husband was drinking, we used to do an awful lot of fighting. I realize now that I was often the one who started it when he came home drunk. The result was always the same. I'd end up boiling mad and helpless to do anything about it.

"'To get rid of my nasty feelings (anger gave me a lot of energy!) I would go out in the backyard and dig. I'd pretend I was digging a grave for my husband; I can't tell you how often I buried him in the backyard! Eventually I had a nice big patch of ground dug up to plant things in. Once the flowers and vegetables began to grow and I didn't dig any more, I got a lot of relief out of pulling weeds and pretending they were his hair. All summer long I used to bring my resentments to Al-Anon meetings—in the form of bright bouquets!

"'You might feel like chopping somebody's head off; chopping a bunch of vegetables for making relish gives you just as much satisfaction—and a good bonus besides.

"'When you feel like "rubbing someone out" you can use that energy to scrub the floor or polish the furniture. And for a really satisfying outlet, one member of my group recommended making bread. You just take that ball of dough and pound and pummel it, pick it up and thump it down on the board and knead it, stretch it as though you were pulling somebody apart—and the result is a batch of delicious, sweet-smelling homemade bread—a nice dividend to get from working off our rages.'

"Any vigorous exercise is a good outlet for anger. Sports like bowling or golf and tennis are great for releasing hostility. In addition to that, concentrating on winning the game keeps our minds free from tormenting thoughts.

"A friend of mine told me she used to have a very sharp tongue, and had developed a socially unacceptable vocabulary which she too often let loose on her children. Someone suggested to her that she give vent to her verbal explosions in the shower, and she tried it. She found she could say anything she wanted to, which gave her a two-way benefit; she'd come out clean in body and mind!

"Another friend says she unloads her anger by writing down all the things she wants to say. If we can do that, we can be as violent as we please—nobody else is going to see it anyway.

"The important thing is that anger is a natural reaction to a frustrating situation. We may not be able to control how we feel but we can control what we do about it. Bottling up anger destroys our peace of mind and often takes physical form in headaches, backaches and other discomforts. Anger should be recognized and released as quickly as possible, and without guilt.

"Of course we must remember never to condemn the alcoholic for being sick, but that doesn't make the things he does any easier to bear. We can pave the way for calm, reasonable communication with him only if we first find healthy outlets for our own negative feelings."

What Do Your Attitudes Communicate?

So much has been said about communicating in words that we may lose sight of another important element in communication, our attitudes, apart from the words we speak.

If the attitude expresses loving awareness or even a reasonable tolerance of the person we're talking to, what we say may fall on receptive ears. If it's an angry accusation or criticism, the situation can't help getting worse. A simple example might be an irritated spouse with a comment to deliver may hurl it at her husband as she would throw a stone at a dog. Her attitude instantly inflames him and a full-fledged row is started.

If she does, in fact, feel for him the contempt she is expressing by her manner of communicating, it may well be a symptom of her own sickness and her need of healing guidance such as Al-Anon provides.

The words we speak may be ever so gentle, but if the "body language" is belligerent it belies the words we are saying. If we assess our behavior honestly, we will see the value of ruling out whatever self-justification may come to mind.

We may suppress things that need to be brought out into the open, because we doubt our own ability to handle them calmly and reasonably; we're afraid the subject is controversial and will set off a quarrel. We learn in time that it is not subjects which are controversial, but the manner in which we communicate about them and the elements of personal blame we add to them in anger.

One night at an Al-Anon meeting a member offered

a problem-question and the members, one after another, were to comment and suggest how the difficulty might have been dealt with.

"When my husband comes home drunk, and in what is surely a blackout, he flies into a rage over almost anything. I don't deny that I'm often the one who gets him started. I'm working on that and I think I've made some progress in avoiding talking at the wrong time and in the wrong way. But last night I had a slip. I made a remark that lit his fuse and in the next five minutes he'd just about wrecked the kitchen and smashed a big hole in the wall.

"This morning at breakfast I didn't say a word and neither did he. He was in the grip of a massive hangover and obviously sick. I felt so sorry for him; my first impulse was to comfort him by trying to make light of the whole thing. I knew I shouldn't do that but I didn't want to hurt him, either. What should I have done, and what do I do now?'

Answers from the group:

No. 1: "If he brings it up, just answer what he asks in a perfectly matter-of-fact way, as though it were understood that he'd done this when he was not himself. If your attitude indicates no blaming, this will be much more effective than going into detail and you'd be less likely to put him on the defensive."

No. 2: "If he doesn't say anything, wait a couple of days and then say, very calmly, 'I think I'll call the plasterer today and get that hole fixed. O.K.? Or do you think we can do it ourselves?'"

No. 3: "I don't agree. I'd leave the hole to remind him of what he did until it bothers him so much he'll have to fix it."

This brought a storm of protest; three hands went up.

"Don't forget the alcoholic is sick!" "We're not supposed to punish; the alcoholic does enough of that for himself!" "That would only make everything worse."

The chairman restored order and went on to the next member who suggested that she say, "'When you get into those uncontrollable rages, I'm always afraid you might hurt one of the children.' He ought to be told what serious consequences his drinking could have."

A man spoke up, "No threats of impending danger ever kept an alcoholic from drinking!"

A long-timer in Al-Anon who had been quietly listening to the discussion, asked to speak. She said,

"It seems to me, the important thing is that we

mustn't take the consequences of the alcoholic's drinking. To me, this adds up to simply—he made the hole in the wall, so he should fix it if he's handy, or pay to have it fixed if he can't or won't fix it himself.

"A similar thing happened to me, only my husband fell on a kitchen chair and broke it. The next day, I said, 'Last night you fell on this and broke it. Will you please have it fixed?' No criticism, no big deal—just plain facts—you did it, you fix it. Because I was calm and didn't berate him, he didn't need to defend himself. He felt bad about what he had done, and was only too happy to have a chance to make up for it."

And finally there came a suggestion that, in any case of violence, the police should be called.

Most of these are reasonable suggestions, but she herself would have to make her decision, based on her relationship with her husband. The common denominator, basic to Al-Anon thinking, is that *there should be no blaming of the alcoholic,* in word or attitude.

Five Guides to Communication

A member once remarked that she had worked out a little set of rules for herself about communicating with her husband, long actively alcoholic, finally solidly sober. She was invited to speak about her self-instructing rules, and this was what she said.

"Discuss, Don't Attack. When my husband was still drinking, this rule saved lots of fights which could only make things worse. But when he was sober, and real personality problems came into focus, I certainly needed this rule. The sober alcoholic is overly sensitive to criticism; and when newly sober, his self-esteem is still fragile. He's so braced for rejection that he imagines it even when it isn't intended. Anything I might say that seems critical of him as a person would make him react emotionally and defensively. If I have a grievance, I just tell him how I feel about it. If it's a minor irritation and it still bothers me I sometimes say: 'I know this is petty, but it gets to me somehow, so I thought you'd want me to tell you about it.'

"Keep the Voice Low and Pleasant. I had lots of experience the other way until I realized that, when feelings run high, voices get high—and then there's trouble. If something I said got a loud-voiced reaction from him, I just left the room. That made him more angry, of course, and for a while he'd follow me and yell: 'Don't you dare walk out on me when I'm talking to you!' But I finally convinced him, in a low

voice, thank goodness, that our shouting days were over, and you'd be surprised at the difference in our home atmosphere!

"Stick to the Subject. When I started to tell him something, it seems I was always using the opportunity to list ten other things I'd been meaning to bring up. At last I sat myself down and said: 'One thing at a time is sufficient. If I confuse the issue, we'll end up fighting about his cousin Joe and my aunt Charlotte.'

"Listen to His Complaints. When it's my turn to be on the receiving end of a complaint, I keep myself receptive to what he's saying, reminding myself that I want to be cool-headed, open-minded, and reasonable. Maybe he's telling me something I need to know that will make me a better person.

"Don't Make Demands. I just state the case without telling him how I think it should be resolved. If he wants to do something about it, he's free to work out a solution of his own. If he doesn't, telling him what to do would be arguing about a solution instead of discussing the problem. By leaving the choice up to him, the door is open for a mutual coming to terms with the problem. Believe me, it was hard work to overcome my thinking that 'my way is the only right way.'"

A Key Word in Communication

This is the story of an Al-Anon member who made an interesting discovery concerning one little word and what it did for her.

"After my husband became sober in A.A., I spent the usual spell on the pink cloud we hear so much about. Although I'd had four years in Al-Anon, my attitude might be summed up this way: 'I've won this battle!'

"I had read all the literature. I rarely missed a meeting. Then why did it take so long, I wonder, for me to see the light? I have finally realized that I never even accepted Step One! I never released my tight grasp on the idea that my sole purpose was to win the battle with my husband and get him sober.

"Nobody could advise the newcomer better than I could. 'Let go!' I would tell her. 'It isn't your problem. He's sick. You have to get over your own flaws of character and learn to let go.'

"I assumed, as so many wives do, that being married to a man put me in charge of him. I felt that he belonged to me and I would somehow make him conform to my way of thinking and living.

"I know now that he might have found help much

sooner if I had only followed the advice I handed out so freely to others.

"So there I was, with a sober husband, triumphant on my pink cloud.

"Little by little, I discovered that I had not conquered him. I didn't change my ways. I tried to tell him how many A.A. meetings to go to; I directed him in a thousand little ways in our daily lives. I resented his resistance, which grew stronger as he devoted himself to the A.A. program. And the more he resisted, the harder I fought.

"Our marriage, as such, had long since foundered on the rock of his alcoholism. I was naturally hoping that we'd get back to a normal way of living now that he was sober. But we didn't. And I couldn't understand why, because I had no real grasp of Al-Anon.

"I blamed his coldness on his interest in women in his group; I grew more and more jealous and suspicious. I monitored his telephone calls, went through his pockets, followed him. Finally I became more frantic and emotionally disturbed than I was when he was drinking. Our rows became pitched battles, and after every one I felt greater despair over the situation.

"They talk about hitting bottom. I hit mine. I realized that getting him sober in A.A. was only the beginning; that something had to be done about me, and I had to do it. In my utter desperation, I turned to Al-Anon like a drowning person going down for the third time. Something opened my mind to insights I had never accepted before:

"First, that my husband was an individual, a distinctly separate person, a child of God—and not my property.

"Second, that my domineering was destroying our relationship, if it had not already been destroyed beyond saving.

"Third, that I would approach my problem very simply and leave the result in God's hands, where it had always belonged.

"I did it with a single word: courtesy.

"People with usually good dispositions have no difficulty being courteous to strangers and friends. It is when our strong emotions are involved that we swing to the limits of the pendulum—extremes of demonstrating affection or disapproval. We are so deeply involved that we treat those closest to us as though they were part of us; when they do things that do not please us, we fight them instead of fighting our own shortcomings.

"Keeping in mind the one word 'courtesy' helped to remind me that my husband is other things besides a husband. He is a man, a person, an individual; he is a man who does a job, earns a living. He is a helping hand to troubled people in A.A. He is a person whose life experience is totally different from mine; he has a mind, a soul, a set of emotions—unique in every way. He is a person to be respected, to be considerate of, to treat always with courtesy.

"From my observation of many marriages, even quite happy ones, there is very little real courtesy, that deference which we owe to every human being, and particularly to those we love. There may be intimacy, togetherness, but what you rarely find is this particular, un-smothering attitude of courtesy.

"It seems like such a little thing, but it worked for me in changing my whole viewpoint about my husband and our marriage. The thought came to me at the time of my greatest need, when a friend lent me a book, *The Prophet*, by Kahlil Gibran, in which he speaks of marriage in this way:

'Let there be spaces in your togetherness. Love one another, but make not a bond of love. Give one another of your bread, but eat not from the same loaf.'

"I have learned that courtesy generates courtesy. It

makes you more pleased with yourself. It makes others, particularly those near to you, reconsider their own attitudes.

"It has worked for me. It may work for you if you have the goodwill and patience to try it."

SEX IN THE
ALCOHOLIC MARRIAGE

As one of the most intimate forms of communication, sex plays an important role in a marriage. Certainly sex problems appear to exist in many alcoholic marriages; the alcoholism either creates problems or exaggerates those which may already be present in one or both partners.

It is self-evident that the quality of a marriage in all its aspects depends upon a wholesome, mutually satisfying sex relationship. The opposite is also true: the sex relationship almost always reflects the feelings of the partners about their marriage as a whole.

In most marriages the needs of the partners almost always differ and require each to make concessions to adjust to the other. If the marriage partners care for one another deeply, each will try to please the other.

Many difficulties are created during the drinking years:

The alcoholic may have grandiose delusions about his sexual prowess and after imbibing may feel a strong desire for sex. If the wife is strongly motivated, so she is able to ignore his condition and still accept his advances, she may be frustrated by his inability to fulfill his or her expectations. She's frustrated and so is he; each blames the other. Every such inconclusive encounter further undermines the marriage.

If his approach is brutally forthright and his wife submits only because she is afraid not to, a condition may result in which she sees her husband and sex as intolerable.

Other wives, repelled by drunken approaches, may refuse outright to submit to the alcoholic's embraces, which again breeds mutual resentment.

The husband's repeated failures may establish impotence which may carry over into sobriety, because fear of failure continues the tension which inhibits him.

If there is a foundation of strong mutual affection and the partners are willing to learn to change their attitudes and actions in relation to sex, there is every hope that the situation will gradually resolve itself.

"Let's Not Talk About It."

In solving the intimate problems of marriage, one of the most difficult obstacles is the unwillingness of one or both partners to sit down to a frank discussion of the matter. This wall between people might be labeled, "Let's not talk about it."

Sex is, for most people, a most difficult topic to talk about. It is so highly charged with emotions of one sort or another—guilt, resentment, bitterness, love—that a reasonable exchange of views and grievances may be virtually impossible. A talk may start out calmly, but as soon as one or the other accuses or reproaches, tempers flare, along with the determination to retaliate. Nothing can be accomplished in this way, which may explain why people give up before they start talking things out and dismiss the whole business with, "Let's not talk about it."

Interviews with many Al-Anon members reveal that this happens frequently. The alcoholic may resist confessing past experiences that may have led to the current impasse. The aggrieved partner wants to know how he or she has failed, and what can be done to restore the marriage status.

This bewilderment shows clearly in such statements as these.

"He's improved in so many ways since he became sober in A.A. He's more than thoughtful and considerate. For the first time he's sending me flowers on occasions; he remembers my sizes and brings me fancy little gifts. It's almost like a courtship, but that's as far as it goes. He hasn't even kissed me in ages. When I try to make an approach to him, even a little one like a peck on the cheek or a pat on the head, he draws away and says, 'Let's not start anything.'

"What am I supposed to think? I'll tell you. Sometimes it seems to me his little attentions are to keep me quiet while he's having an affair with someone else. I'm afraid something about me repels him. Other times I think he's sorry for me and wants to comfort me because he can't bring himself to any intimacies with me.

"I asked a friend who's a marriage counselor (my husband just wouldn't go with me) what it's all about and she said, 'He's probably deeply troubled by guilt over the way he treated you when he was still drinking. Not knowing him, I can't tell you what to do about the situation, but it might help if you could get him to have a frank talk about it. Don't make any secret of the fact that you're interested in sex and that you want him. Don't be coy about it. You'll have to convince him that you aren't concerned about anything that happened in his drinking past. Explain to him that now that you've had a couple of years in Al-Anon you realize how much you were at fault in the many fights and difficulties that happened while he was drinking.'"

Another attractive young wife, bewildered by her husband's coldness, tried the age-old trick of being a temptress. She had noticed that the women he usually found occasion to chat with were the more obvious glamour types, flaming red-heads or blondes, with effective makeup, an aura of perfume, and seductively designed clothes.

Since in her own personality she was rather conservative, always immaculately groomed, and charmingly dressed, she limited her first attempt to a new hair style, a slight increase in makeup and brighter clothes colors than usual.

The effect on her husband, once he did notice

the change, was one of irritation, "Who are you on the make for, dressed up like that?" Naturally she was hurt, since she couldn't imagine why he liked eye-stopping effects in other women and not in her.

At home she tried other ways to call his attention to the fact that she was a woman, a loving wife who wanted his husbandly attentions and intimacies. She took perfumed bubble baths, donned alluring negligees. That didn't work either. The first attempts were greeted with silence. The final one brought an outburst, "Oh, for Pete's sake, get dressed and let's go out."

What is a woman in this position to do? Her husband refuses to go to a psychiatrist or to a marriage counselor. He will not discuss sex, nor the reasons for the absence of it. His wife refuses other outlets. She is in love with her husband and wants no one else, although she has had several opportunities. She feels there is no choice but to accept the difficult continence that has been forced upon her. And like most of those interviewed, her shy attempts to bring the subject up were drowned out with, "Let's not talk about it!"

It never occurred to her that he set her far apart and

above the women he found it casually amusing to talk to. She didn't realize that he wanted her exactly as she was, someone to be proud of and to adore. But at a distance! It just couldn't have occurred to her that his inability to make love to her stemmed from his own feeling of unworthiness.

There was another woman who found herself in a similar situation. While her husband was drinking, she often felt such a revulsion at his approaches that she flatly refused to have anything to do with him. She knew some of the instances in which this drove him to other beds, and although she was bitter about that, she realized that she had at least a share in making it possible or necessary for him to turn to other women. Then came sobriety, with the customary pink-cloud elation. Although we learn in Al-Anon to be wary in that first period of success, knowing that new difficulties are lying in wait, she was happy for the first time in years. As his health and activity improved, he devoted much time and energy to rebuilding his business. He seemed to delight in being able to provide his family with much better living than when he was drinking. His sole activity outside his business was attending A.A. meetings and talking with A.A. friends.

As this happy way of life went on, the wife supposed that resumption of their sex life would follow in due course. But it didn't. He seemed to have adopted a monastic discipline which ruled out all pleasures, even marital. He appeared to be wholly concentrated on developing his own personal perfection as he saw it, in which sex was something to be offered up as a restitution for his past sins.

His wife somehow grasped this motivation and made a realistic appraisal of her own role. Having refused to sleep with him when he was drinking, she did not entirely blame him for his present attitude, whatever its actual cause might be.

She did everything she could to please him, to make him feel he was once more head of the household. Still no change.

As months went by, tensions increased. She carefully examined all the alternatives. She didn't want to give up her husband, but she wanted him to *be* a husband; yet she had no intention of continuing this ascetic life which came with sobriety.

One morning, at breakfast, having come to a decision during a sleepless night, she announced,

"Now, my friend, you and I are going to straighten out this problem of our non-existent sex life."

"Let's not talk about it!" he protested, "It just isn't something you drag out into the open."

"Oh, yes it is. If it's important enough to threaten the unity of this family, we're going to find out what's wrong. I can tell you that I'm not going on this way. I'm a woman, a wife, with normal desires for intimacy with my husband, whom, by the way, I dearly love. I want to know whether it's something about me that makes me unacceptable, or whether something's irking you. If it's sickness—emotional or physical—there are steps to be taken, if you want to. But we have to get this thing cleared up. I know it isn't romantic or seductive to put cards on the table like this—but that can come later, when we understand what's wrong.'

After a long silence, her husband finally explained that it was his feeling of guilt about his drinking, his neglect of his work and the consequences to his family and, finally, the several casual affairs that involved actual sex relationships with others.

"I just can't get over these things—not right away. But I can tell you that you've made me feel a lot better by letting me know that you really want me, and care about me even though I was such a heel for so long."

This young woman reports that she now knows what honeymoons are like, though she never did before, even the very first!

An A.A. Member's View

As the previous section indicates, the spouse of an alcoholic is confused and bewildered by the sex maladjustment.

Although she may have learned in Al-Anon that no one can understand the motivations of another person, she is baffled by her inability to understand "what's happened to my marriage."

The following explanation, by an alcoholic who has long been sober in A.A., is offered as one man's view of the situation. It may be typical, it may not be, but it does help to throw some light on the attitude of the sobered alcoholic.

"I have talked to many people in A.A. about marriage problems and what causes them, and what I have to say here is sort of a composite of what I know from my own experience and what I have heard from others.

"The arrested alcoholic's sex problem seems to stem from a conditioning which is so complicated that it is difficult, if not impossible, to explain even the versions which I do know about. I want to emphasize that my conclusions would not apply generally, but only in certain situations.

"I think we might often get a clearer picture of the trouble if we gave more consideration to the original reasons for the marriage, and how the basic personalities of the partners react to one another. For example, one known characteristic of the alcoholic is dependency. He tends to look for a mothering wife, someone he can lean on. When he finds a woman he wants to marry, it is therefore one who has a strongly developed mother instinct, and who, in turn, wants a man to baby and protect.

"It might seem that two such people would actually complement each other and so make an ideal marriage, since each would provide what the other one needs. But a mother-child relationship is, to begin with, an unsound basis for an adult marriage. Apart from the alcoholism, they're already headed for trouble.

"Then when the alcoholism accentuates the drinker's dependency, and the burden becomes too much for the wife, she takes refuge in self-pity and resentment.

"Her attitude toward him, unconscious though it may be, is not geared to transforming him into a man of responsibility. His attitude toward her, as his drinking becomes more and more compulsive, is an unconscious disappointment that 'mama' has failed him by expecting him to be grown up.

"When such a man finds sobriety in A.A. and really takes hold of the Twelve Step program, it is bound to create changes in their marriage relationship that neither one is prepared for. He becomes determined to grow up, to assume his responsibilities, to make his sobriety count in terms of adult living. He wants to overcome his dependency, leave the 'mama' business behind him. But this wish cannot, of itself, change his wife's attitude or behavior, and the rift between them grows wider. They can never return to the early phases of their marriage, for he no longer wants to lean on her.

"Since his wife has been to him, from the beginning, a mother figure, he may also have deeply rooted feelings about his marital relations with her, and this would tend to make him shy away from her as a marriage partner.

"I am not saying that any of this is clearly realized by the people involved in such a situation, but it is there, and it can operate to change their relationship into something that neither of them finds tolerable.

"Another way of trying to visualize this difficulty is to realize that the alcoholic is basically insecure and therefore seeks a partner who is stronger. Call it a mother figure, a father figure or a god figure, he will, in his mind, build it up to what his need demands and carefully protect this image from anything that might expose its weakness or reduce its importance in his mind.

"I have known many men alcoholics who were so rugged and masculine that no one would ever imagine their being dependent, especially on a woman. They might complain about their wives in superficial ways—'she's a lousy cook, a shiftless housekeeper, does nothing but go to the movies and play cards'—but such complaints are offered only as an excuse for drinking and so are meaningless. They never speak of their wives as being weak, helpless, or stupid. This they would never do, because they'd be destroying the bulwark of protection their wives represent to them, their shield against a menacing world.

"The alcoholic often attributes to his spouse characteristics and attitudes that exist only in his mind.

He may place her in a position of super-ego, a kind of deity, and not a gentle and forgiving one, but a punishing one. This, too, meets a desperate need in him. Overcome by his terrible guilt, the alcoholic actually craves punishment because he wants his guilt alleviated. And when she does denounce him, rail at him, fight with him, the 'culprit' feels a sense of relief, as though he had paid for his sins. In this way, she plays right into his hands and makes it possible for him to excuse his continued drinking. She, at the same time, has relieved her pent-up feelings about his irresponsibility and neglect, and in this unhealthy interaction, alcoholic marriages often go on year after year with neither one making any effort to break out of this destructive pattern.

"If she is gentle and long-suffering, her image increases his guilt and drives him still further in his search for oblivion through alcohol.

"But in either case, and whether he is drinking or has become sober, he has unwittingly forced her to stay in place on a pedestal where he feels her to be unapproachable. Being alcoholics, we feel like earthy clods who have no right to make love to a person in that exalted position in our lives. In some cases, it's a matter of feeling that we have partaken of the pleasures of the 'devil' and therefore do not feel at ease with an 'angel.'

"Sometimes, because of sordid entanglements that may happen during blackouts, or even through the warped judgment that alcoholic elation brings about, he may equate alcohol and sex as evils, and once he has taken steps to overcome his addiction to alcohol, he also shies away from sex.

"In other cases, difficulties in making sexual adjustments after sobriety may be due to a too-rigid attitude on the part of the spouse. Let's say a crisis has brought the alcoholic into A.A. He begins to correct his character faults, he is learning to take a more realistic view of life. As he struggles to make this slow climb back to sanity, his wife may continue to bring up his past faults. She may resent his dedication to A.A. that takes him to so many meetings. In other words, he is growing while she is stuck with all the old resentments that keep her angry and confused.

"It seems to me the only hope of ironing out difficulties of this kind is for the spouse to turn to Al-Anon where she can learn to understand her situation more clearly, and how to overcome the faults in her that contributed to the rift in their marriage. Once she discovers that she was not entirely blameless in all that has happened, they can go forward together and establish a relationship of mutual respect, tolerance, and affection."

Whose "Fault" Is It?

When a marriage is beset by sex problems, the first thing to overcome is the idea that either of the partners is at fault. Both are unquestionably miserable, both blindly seeking answers, and both invariably blame each other for what's wrong with the relationship. This puts both partners on the defensive but does nothing to solve the problem. In fact, it can seriously aggravate the situation. It is better to think of the marriage *relationship* as needing improvement.

Without our realizing it, our own destructive attitudes may contribute to our sex problems. Among the attitudes which have come to light in conversations among Al-Anon members are these.

THE DOUBTER: If the wife still has uneasy doubts about her husband—whether he will really stay sober and be a dependable partner in the marriage—this may also create difficulties in the sexual area. Her long experience during the drinking years may have left her fearful of being hurt. She cannot easily let go and put herself completely in another's care for even a moment. Such doubt can impair a woman's ability to relate sexually to her spouse.

Such problems often disappear as the marriage itself improves and the partners relate to each other with growing confidence.

THE DOMINATOR: For the woman who resists releasing the reins and allowing her husband to resume his responsibilities, the sex arena may be her last stronghold for asserting herself.

What a cruel and subtle way it is to tell him he isn't the boss when she refuses to react pleasurably to his sexual advances! What she is really saying, as she unconsciously takes out her frustration on him is, "You may think you're the boss, but we both know how inadequate you are. Here in the bedroom, where your masculinity is on the line, you can't control me and get the response you want."

This destructive attitude creates a hostility that strikes at the very roots of the marriage.

A similar experience was brought up at an Al-Anon meeting and when the members challenged the wife's attitude, she said she had not even been aware that her reason was a subconscious resistance to reinstating her husband as head of the family. After her attitude was made clear to her, she was able to bring about a change in herself, and some months later she reported to her Sponsor that all was now going well.

THE PUNISHER: This is perhaps the most common reaction to the alcoholic, "I'm good, he's bad; he deserves to be punished," or, "He makes me suffer so I'll make him suffer." Punishment and retaliation help nobody; they prolong the active alcoholism, and widen the rift in the marriage.

Everything that is written and said, or conveyed in any way in the Al-Anon program, points up the fact that *nobody has a right to punish anyone else.* Add to that the alcoholic's suffering from his illness, and the punisher has little or nothing to justify her behavior.

A member confessed at an Al-Anon meeting, "I found it so hard to get rid of the idea of alcoholism as a moral problem. I just couldn't help seeing my husband as a bad, deliberately bad, person who could be good if he only wanted to.

"I rewarded and punished as though I were God. One of my major weapons was sex. If he was 'behaving' I would sleep with him; when he was bad I denied him sex even though I actually felt no personal revulsion for him. I withheld sex even when I was in the mood myself, just to punish him.

"I can understand a wife's being disgusted with a drunk and not wanting to have any physical contact with him. That's a valid reason for refusing him; but I had no such excuse."

THE MARTYR: "So you suffer," commented an Al-Anon member to another who had just bemoaned her sorry lot in life. "O.K., you cook and clean and take care of the children. You do your work, your husband's chores and volunteer for countless neighborhood activities. Could it be you like the excuse of being 'too tired' when your husband is ready for sex? And when you say you feel 'used' by his sex requirements, don't you see that's just how you feel about your whole life?

"All of us feel sorry for ourselves at times, especially if we've been through the fire of living with an active drinker, but your husband is sober now and you ought to be learning how to get rid of some of the attitudes that keep you from living fully and enjoying every day. So how about working out of this martyr role and getting some fun out of life!"

THE DEMANDER: In this case it's the sober alcoholic husband who seems to be creating a problem for his wife. Here's how she told her story to her Sponsor.

"My husband was always very demanding about sex. Seemed to me he talked about it constantly. He'd approach me when I was tired, sick, troubled; he'd even insist on immediate action when we had company or it was time to put the children to bed.

"I felt it was unreasonable, but still I thought I was at fault because I couldn't see having sex as often as he wanted to. He insisted I was frigid and the more he nagged about it, the less I was inclined to give in. The cooler I got, the hotter the issue became.

"Finally I was so repelled by his constant demands that I thought I really was frigid. I couldn't enjoy sex any more and I didn't even want to hear about it.

"One night at an Al-Anon meeting, the speaker was

a doctor. Someone asked a question that related to a problem a lot like mine. His answer certainly was a complete shock—I couldn't believe it!

"He suggested that the woman pretend she had suddenly become very much interested in sex, and to urge it on her husband at every possible opportunity.

"His theory was that some men who make such a big issue of sex are worried about their own manhood—they're trying to prove something to reassure themselves. It doesn't matter that they're refused so often—in fact they count on it. Their constant unrealistic demands are used to convince themselves that they're real he-males with powerful sex urges.

"Deciding I had nothing to lose, I tried it. I read books on sex and discussed them with my husband. I sort of acted toward him as though he were a toy for my special amusement. Well! He started watching the Late Show on TV, being very tired at bedtime, acting cool when I approached him. I think I must have scared him!

"Since then we've had a good understanding about the whole thing and have found a pleasant middle ground that's delightful for both of us."

THE STORY OF
DONNA AND DON

In general, the foregoing section discussed sex problems as they relate to alcoholism. But we should be aware that there may be other circumstances that affect the situation, often going back far into childhood. The following story illustrates the idea; although alcoholism was, in fact, involved, there were other, more difficult complications.

Donna grew up in a happy, affectionate family. Her view of home life came from a dependable, provident, good-natured father and a warm, loving mother. When Donna anticipated marriage to Donald, a charming man she had met at college, she could imagine it only as more of the same sort of life, with herself in the wife and mother role.

Donald was the son of a highly successful, hard-drinking father, and an indifferent mother who used the family's ample means to enjoy life on her own terms. Donald grew up with a succession of nurses and tutors until he was sent away to an expensive prep school at 14. Every material wish was fulfilled from earliest childhood—his parents found it more convenient to indulge him than bother with him. Lack of parental love resulted in character and personality distortion which first showed itself in his drinking at prep school and college. His family wasn't particularly worried when he got into scrapes; they blamed it on the high spirits of youth, and always bailed him out of his trouble, whether it meant transferring him to another college after expulsion, or buying him a new car to replace one he had smashed up.

Donald and Donna fell in love. They had many interests in common and got along beautifully except when Donna reproached him for drinking too much. She didn't really blame him; she thought it was due to his having been misled by the kind of fellows with whom he associated. Alcohol, as such, had no terrors for her; in her home the occasional cocktail party was fun, and there was usually a glass of wine with dinner.

And so they were married. Don promised Donna faithfully he would limit his drinking. Because he already had secret misgivings about his ability to control it, he resolved to stop drinking entirely after their honeymoon.

The trip to Europe was an ecstatic affair; both enjoyed the shipboard parties, their travels in foreign countries, and the general gaiety, always heightened by a few drinks. As for their sexual adjustment, that was ecstatic, too. This was clearly a marriage that would last.

On their return, Don went eagerly and earnestly to work. He had decided that drinking would be no part of his perfect life with Donna, and she readily agreed. Fired with ambition to make a success that would match his father's, he worked long, hard hours. His work began to absorb all his time and attention. Donna was bewildered at his lack of interest in her, but firmly resolved to accept the situation because she realized the exhausting demands of his work. After all, she reasoned, he was building a career for them.

But as time went on, the situation became strained; Donna was increasingly nervous and tense as his indifference to her continued. Verbally he assured her how much he loved her, and that "everything will be all right soon." But it wasn't all right. Donna began to suspect him of having other interests, and quarrels and accusations widened the rift between them.

One evening, in the midst of a bitter quarrel, Don suddenly put on his hat and coat and left the house. When he came back after midnight, he had evidently been drinking, and Donna was filled with shame and remorse at having "driven him to it".

He reassured her, explained that he thought much of their trouble was due to his tensions. "And so," he told Donna, "I thought a few drinks would relax me. What we ought to do, both of us," he went on, "is to have a couple of cocktails in the evenings. Then we'd both take a rosier view."

Donna agreed to this suggestion, the honeymoon status was resumed, and the rift healed. And both were happy again in the resumption of their sex life.

As Don's drinking again went beyond bounds, his behavior revolted her, and then it was she who resisted his advances, and another crisis was underway.

Again Don tried a difficult, self-imposed sobriety, and again came the tensions created by his aversion to sex when he was sober.

A long course of psychiatric analysis only helped to uncover some of the causes of the problems, but did nothing to correct them.

Don finally found his solution in A.A., but not before Donna had left him.

A later report from a friend of this couple indicated that Donna had joined Al-Anon and the two were finally reunited.

HOW ONE WOMAN SOLVED
HER MARRIAGE PROBLEM

Some time ago there appeared in *The A.A. Grapevine* the first of a series of articles called "Seven Choices for Mature Living." The author, Robert K. Greenleaf, had been Director of Personnel Research for a large corporation. As part of his work, he had occasion to give a course for executives.

The teaching procedure included having his students make a complete analysis of their jobs and an honest appraisal of their attitudes toward them.

During the first of the three annual sessions, one of his best students, a mature woman executive, did an outstanding analysis of her job and her performance in it. Self-evaluation was the important thing.

When she returned for the second year's session, Mr. Greenleaf heard her remarkable story.

After the first year's class, she had taken an overnight train back to her home. Once settled in the train, she began to study the analysis board on which she had so thoroughly reviewed the facts about herself and her work. She wondered whether a similar analysis of her personal problem—her marriage—might not be helped by an honest dissection of all the factors that made it such a problem.

Twenty-five years of a marriage that was no marriage; each partner engrossed in work; an apartment that was not a home, but merely a place where both lived, and a marriage relationship that was, on the human level, a dismal failure.

"As I sat there looking at my business analysis," she told Mr. Greenleaf, "I wondered if I couldn't apply the same procedure to this problem of mine. I tried it. I sat up all night working on it, and the next morning, I knew what to do about my marriage and I was determined to do it."

She listed and described the attitudes that each partner would need to hold in order to make it a successful marriage. When she had completed the analysis, she received the insight she was searching for. She realized that if a marriage relationship were to change, *the one who first saw the kind of attitudes required* had the obligation to hold these attitudes and behave accordingly.

"This," said Mr. Greenleaf in the article, "is the root of responsibility, to respond to the obligation which is imposed upon the one who sees the opportunity to instigate a change. Obviously the partner who does not see it cannot respond to the obligation."

The woman who had reached this determination resolved "that I would hold and act upon these attitudes, not knowing, but trusting that my husband would respond. Fortunately I had the tenacity to continue this for quite a time without any response from him. But now, finally, after a year, we have a really good marriage."

Reading between the lines we see that this woman shouldered the entire responsibility for correcting whatever was wrong with the marriage. She did not put it on the basis of: "If he does this, I'll do that." She acted according to a pattern she had set for herself—she did not react. She was totally motivated by a desire to restore to health a relationship that was in serious difficulty, and she did not allow herself to be deflected from her course by anything that happened.

"This," said Mr. Greenleaf in conclusion, "is a success story. It might not have turned out this way. But no matter; it was a character-building, responsible act by the person who performed it. And either way, she is a healthier, saner, more whole person for having acted responsibly."

The interesting thing about this story is that the heroine of it used Al-Anon principles in solving her problem. Al-Anon teaches us to look to ourselves and our own shortcomings. It tells us to stop aggravating our difficulties, and to practice detachment from the problem. The Steps and the slogans are full of suggestions that would lead us along the same path this woman took with such wisdom and honesty.

Many of us have learned, in Al-Anon, to live with an alcoholic problem in serenity and peace of mind. In the same way we can solve the problems of marriage maladjustments by first taking a long look at ourselves, our behavior, our reactions.

FOR THE HUSBAND
OF AN ALCOHOLIC

It is deeply disturbing for a man to realize that his wife is an alcoholic. When he chose her as a marriage partner he was, in effect, telling the world that he had a wife to be proud of, a choice that reflected credit on his taste and judgment. When he finally faces the fact that his wife cannot control her drinking, he feels let down; he thinks the shame is somehow his, and that he may even be responsible for her addiction.

His masculine pride won't let him expose his problem by asking for help, even when he knows such help is available. It seems somehow to be his personal failure, which he feels violates the accepted standards of society. Actually those standards are purely arbitrary and are constantly undergoing change. The idea that the man is the dominant factor, and therefore responsible for everything that takes place in his family, is fast being replaced by the more realistic view that husband and wife are two distinct individuals, equal in status and each responsible for himself.

Although many still find it difficult to admit that "My wife has a problem with alcohol," seeking help is the most sensible course anyone can take, and the kindest to the alcoholic as well. Thousands of men who are members of Al-Anon would assure them of this.

The alcoholic cannot be helped unless she desires help. But a marriage can be improved even if only one of the partners takes steps to understand the problem and do something about it. That person must be the one who recognizes the need.

He may gradually be forced to take over all his wife's responsibilities and be father, mother, breadwinner, and housekeeper. His confused emotions range from self-pity to anger at his wife for not realizing what her alcoholism is doing to her family. He may bribe, threaten, hide liquor, withhold money, and sometimes even resort to blows—all to no avail. His helplessness to make her be what he wants her to be, his own failure to handle the situation more effectively, combined with the pressures of his practical problems, keep him on a crisis course. If, in desperation, he finally turns to Al-Anon he learns that others have found the way out of similar problems.

Al-Anon holds out no promise of sobriety for the alcoholic and no magic solution. What Al-Anon does offer for the taking is the assurance that things can get better. He meets other men who have found a way to a better way of life.

He is at once reassured by learning that, no matter what his wife says, he did not cause her drinking problem. This alone means one less burden for him to carry.

Then he finds out that there are better ways to deal with the alcoholic, and that most of the ways he has tried are futile. He learns which attitudes are helpful, and which are destructive; he discovers how to keep his frustrations from becoming ugly resentments. His confusions are resolved by rational explanations and information. Gradually, the problems that seemed insurmountable begin, through his own changing point of view, to clear up.

Once a man's wife has found sobriety, he is likely to fall into the error of expecting miracles of change, in attitude, action, and personality. If he continues with the support of the Al-Anon program, he will understand that it takes a long time for the alcoholic to adjust to a new way of life without the crutch of the bottle.

He may even resent changes in her; her concern for her appearance, a new interest in grooming and clothes, her need for the many A.A. meetings which keep her out evenings, and her many new A.A. friends who are helping her keep sober. She now has something in which he has no part and his dissatisfaction may even have a large element of envy or jealousy.

At an Al-Anon meeting a member spoke of such an experience during the early months of his wife's sobriety.

"She went to meetings every night; her A.A. Sponsor said it had to be that way. At first I thought it was a small price to pay for her sobriety, my staying at home alone night after night. But as new problems arose, I began to resent the whole situation and in time I got pretty bitter about the importance of A.A. in her life. Off she'd go every evening, looking better than she had in all the drinking years, and I was deprived of her company. Oh, I was good and sorry for myself! I don't know what would have happened to our marriage if I hadn't met Hank, who'd been coming to this group for three years. He talked me into trying it, and I have found something I never dreamed was possible: a life of my own, friends with a common interest, healthy interchange of ideas about our problems. Al-Anon has filled a void in my life and given me a new perspective on my marriage. My present experience in growth parallels my wife's which, as we say in Al-Anon, draws us closer together."

*   *   *

And here are the words of another man who discovered his need for Al-Anon after his wife became sober.

"Since I did not have the benefit of Al-Anon during my wife's active drinking years, I can discuss only what Al-Anon has meant in my own slow and often painful recovery, and how much it helps in living with the sober alcoholic.

"For a long time after I came into Al-Anon I thought I had accepted the First Step: that I was 'powerless over alcohol' and over the person afflicted with alcoholism. I desperately wanted to make progress with the program as given in the Twelve Steps, and yet I was getting nowhere. I had hit a stumbling block I couldn't figure out. Late one night, after long discussion and many cups of coffee, a wise longtimer in Al-Anon quietly pointed out to me where I had gone astray: I had never really accepted the whole First Step. I was continuing to blame everything that had happened and was still happening, on that one thing I was powerless over—alcohol. But there I stopped, because I had a complete mental block about the second and most vital part of the Step: 'that our lives had become unmanageable.' I was willing to admit that the lives of my wife and others were unmanageable, but not mine, oh no!

"During her drinking years I developed a certain pattern of living for myself which, unconsciously, I based on my living with an active drinker for the rest of my life. If anyone had asked me, I would have said, with a touch of self-pity in my voice, that I was managing my life excellently considering the conditions under which I was living. Actually I had withdrawn into my shell, and my only contacts were those made necessary by my business.

"When my wife achieved sobriety and began to build it up one day at a time, I wasn't ready for the change. Her sobriety, I thought, was what I had worked, wanted, hoped and prayed for above all, and that if it came, it would be the answer to all our problems. Actually, sobriety was not the answer or the end; it was only the beginning. Sobriety, strangely enough, eventually created problems and situations that hadn't existed during her drinking period. It was only after she was sober in A.A. that the extent of my own sickness became apparent but it took me a long time to recognize and acknowledge this.

"I never want to forget that the sober alcoholic is still and always will be an alcoholic. When sobriety comes, we expect too much, too great a change, because of our own complacency, impatience, and lack of tolerance and understanding. We think the alcoholic should behave 'normally,' whatever that is. The spouse of the alcoholic, being sick too, reacts differently to the behavior of the drinking alcoholic than to the sober one. He builds up resentments toward situations that would not have troubled him during the drinking period.

"I resented the newfound sobriety, although I wasn't even aware of this. I resented the alcoholic's trying to resume her proper place in the home, and as part of the marriage team, after so many years. In short, the sober alcoholic was recovering day by day, while I was still sick and getting sicker.

"The change from years of daily drinking to sobriety is probably the most radical a person can experience. But just because the alcoholic wife becomes sober there isn't an automatic corresponding change in her spouse.

"I certainly don't mean to imply that sobriety is not desirable or that I was better off when my wife was drinking. As time goes on, and with the help of Al-Anon, I am learning each day to put things into proper perspective and to see more clearly what happened to me and how I behaved. It is only now that I am able to see that my wife's becoming sober did not make me well—nor could it. Expecting this is one of the major errors the spouse of an alcoholic makes. We relate too closely to what the alcoholic does and doesn't do, and let these things influence our thinking, actions and reactions.

"I now have a goal I can see clearly; and the program with which to work toward it. It is my guide to self-improvement, comfort, and a better way of life.

"One of these days I hope to be able to make amends to all those I harmed, including my alcoholic wife—and myself. I can only try."

HOW THE TWELVE STEPS APPLY
TO MARRIAGE PROBLEMS

Here are some questions to ask yourself about
your marriage, suggested by the Twelve Steps of
Al-Anon.

STEP ONE

We admitted we were powerless over alcohol—
that our lives had become unmanageable.

Have I really accepted the fact that I cannot control
another person's drinking? Am I willing to carry this
acceptance a step further and admit I am powerless
over anyone but myself?

Do I realize that the alcoholic is an individual? That
the alcoholic has habit patterns, characteristics, and
ways of reacting to daily happenings that are different
from mine and from other people's?

Can I believe that these individual qualities were established by the alcoholic's heritage, early training, experiences, and contacts throughout life?

Can I realize that my trying to change the alcoholic only brings resistance in the form of hostility or hidden resentment?

If I do realize this, can I justify my criticism and condemnation of the alcoholic?

Will I try to overcome my resentment that arises when the alcoholic refuses to be and do what I want the alcoholic to?

Will I try to teach myself to stop trying to make the alcoholic over?

> I will remind myself, hour after hour each day, that I am powerless over anyone else, that I can live no life but my own. Changing *myself* for the better is the only way I can find peace and serenity.
>
> I will remind myself that a change in my attitude can smooth out many difficulties.

STEP TWO

*Came to believe that a Power greater than ourselves
could restore us to sanity.*

Can I admit that many of the things I said and
did while my spouse was drinking really were not
sane?

Am I willing to recognize that the alcoholic situation, with its disappointments, battles, frustrations,
money shortages, and constant fears, actually did
affect my sanity?

Can I accept the fact that, with my own human
powers, I am not able to handle everything com-
petently and wisely? Or do I still think that I am
capable of making right decisions about everything?

Do I imagine that no one else is going through the
torments of an alcoholic marriage with its lack of
security, thoughtfulness, tenderness, admiration, and
love?

Do I yield to despair because I feel I am trapped in
a situation in which I am nothing but a drudge and a

crutch?

Then can I "come to believe" that I do need help in straightening out my thinking and developing a rational frame of mind?

> I accept the fact that I need help in being restored to sanity, and that I cannot achieve this without help.

STEP THREE

Made a decision to turn our will and our lives over to the care of God as we understood Him.

Am I ready to make this decision to let go, and let God take a hand in managing my life?

Am I ready to keep hands off situations created by others, no matter what happens?

Or will I still try to intercept each problem, and try to handle it myself?

Do I understand that I am turning over to the care of God only my own life and will, only my own problem—nobody else's?

Can I resolve not to "play God" in relation to anyone else, but allow others to work out their own salvation, just as I am trying to work out mine?

Will I guard against the tendency to let my self-will take over again, allowing my old patterns of thought and action to bring confusion and despair back into my daily life?

Will I try to express God's will in all my actions and words toward others, and particularly toward the alcoholic whose sufferings I cannot understand or share?

> I have done my best and it isn't good enough. Now I know I need the help of a Power greater than my own. I know that help is waiting only for my acceptance, waiting for me to say, "Not my will but Thine be done."
>
> Once I have decided to turn my life and my will over to "God as I understand Him," I know I must empty my mind and my feelings of fear of what may happen, of the shame and embarrassment over the behavior of others.
>
> In everything I do, I will try to reflect the light and the wisdom that will come to me through my surrender to my Higher Power.

STEP FOUR

Made a searching and fearless moral inventory of ourselves.

Recognizing that I am not entirely without fault in my unhappy situation, I ask myself:

Have I allowed myself to harbor resentment?

Am I a victim of self-pity, increasing the agony by magnifying it in my mind?

Do I criticize and condemn?

Do I dedicate myself to the job that is mine—my work, my home, my family, my self-development?

Do I feel compelled to assume responsibilities that belong to another person, or to shame another, either to show what a martyr I am or because I fear the disapproval of friends and relatives and neighbors?

Do I punish and retaliate for real or imagined hurts?

Do I expose my sick spouse to the contempt of others?

Do I give in to despair, to a hopeless "What's the use?" attitude?

Do I lie to cover up for the alcoholic?

Do I take out my frustrations on my children and others?

Do I allow my mind to dwell on the alcoholic's shortcomings instead of my own?

Can I learn to keep aware of my dignity and grace which are the birthright of every child of God?

Day by day I will try to overcome my own faults and mistakes, knowing that this course of thinking, acting and speaking alone can work toward a solution of my problems.

STEP FIVE

Admitted to God, to ourselves, and to another human being the exact nature of our wrongs.

Do I see the importance of admitting my faults, privately to God in my meditation and prayer and openly to another person whom I respect and trust to keep my confidences?

Knowing that no one is perfect, can I concede that I am not perfect either?

Do I realize that the use of this Step will help me to recognize and deal with my own shortcoming?

Isn't this Step essential for improvement, since I know that admitting my shortcomings only to myself would soon leave me open to excusing them and doing nothing constructive about them?

Do I understand the healing relief of honest acknowledgment of faults?

When I concentrate on my personal progress, the difficulties over which I have no control will iron themselves out.

STEP SIX

Were entirely ready to have God remove all these defects of character.

Can I see that character defects are most easily removed by replacing them with healthy, constructive traits and actions?

Do I realize that God does not remove a fault to produce a vacuum, but to make room for one of His ideas: love, kindness, tolerance?

Wouldn't I like myself better if I switched off critical thoughts of something somebody did and replaced them with admiration for something nice about that person?

Do I know in my innermost heart that I could accept the good God has available for me if I were not propelled into resistance by my own self-will?

Do I know that the words "entirely ready" mean my own complete surrender to God's will?

Do I realize that such surrender is not weakness, but strength that will reinforce my courage and confidence?

In the humility of surrender we find ourselves. We become able to see our God-given good qualities, too.

All progress must grow from a seed of self-appreciation which is as far removed from conceit and pride as day is from night.

Let me realize too, that self-doubt and self-hate are defects of character that hinder my growth.

STEP SEVEN

Humbly asked Him to remove our shortcomings.

Am I really ready to have my shortcomings removed?

Or do I cling to some of my favorite ones, those I think are justified by circumstances?

Do I know they cannot be removed until I am ready, that while I have any secret reservations, or even unrealized ones, I cannot be ready to be helped toward my goal of a full, serene life?

Have I reached a point of being truly humble?

Is it only my mind that is ready, or do I ardently wish, from my heart, to be taught how to live in the light?

Quiet and meek as the tone of this Step appears, do I recognize it as an instrument of stupendous power to change my life?

How soon will I learn to put it to my use?

Humility is basically a realization of our relationship to our Higher Power.

STEP EIGHT

*Made a list of all persons we had harmed, and
became willing to make amends to them all.*

As I review the injustices I have done to others, do I
see a significant pattern that indicated a character flaw
I ought to try to correct? A tendency to gossip, to criticize? A habit of taking offense readily and causing
dissension? A quick temper that makes words erupt
without my thinking of the effect they will have?

Do I see this Step as a statement of my responsibility, a suggestion that I have now become strong
enough to make restitution for what I have done to
others?

Shouldn't I regard it as an opportunity to make
good, to unburden myself of whatever lingering feelings of guilt may still be troubling me?

Am I eager to hold up my head and say, "I have
fulfilled my obligations"?

When willingness to make amends can mean so
much to me, to my peace of mind, why do I hesitate?

Let me remind myself, "I am willing to make
amends," but more than that, I am willing to learn to

be tolerant and generous in my views about other people, and to consider their feelings and weaknesses.

STEP NINE

Made direct amends to such people wherever possible, except when to do so would injure them or others.

How can I make a fresh start unless I acknowledge the actions and words I regret, and make amends for them in the best way I can?

Do I realize what a basic and wholesome healing it can be for me to clear the slate of guilt for hurt I have done to others?

Shouldn't I start by making amends to those in my immediate family, and especially the alcoholic, for my impatience, reproaches, and criticisms which probably rose out of my own hysteria and confusion?

If I have become estranged from friends and relatives, wouldn't now be a good time to heal these separations by making friendly overtures without reserve, and without any attempt to fix blame for what occurred?

Wouldn't I reap rich rewards in comfort and peace of mind by humbly acknowledging whatever wrongs I have done, and making up for them in full?

Before I start making amends, I will make sure there is no lingering residue of resentment or self-righteousness left in me.

Let me remember that the reason for making amends is to free my own mind of uneasiness; there is no need to review each matter to see who is at fault.

STEP TEN

Continued to take personal inventory and when we were wrong promptly admitted it.

Do I review daily the things I have said or done that I wish I hadn't as well as those I feel good about?

Do I learn from these daily inventories, so that each day is better for me than the one before?

Do I try to avoid making judgments based only on my own point of view, which may not be entirely correct?

Do I understand that taking "personal inventory" means only my inventory, and not that of the alcoholic or anyone else?

Do I always remember to include in my personal inventory the things that are good about me, relishing the thought of a kindness I have done, help I have given to someone? Or generously excusing another's fault?

> Daily vigilance will turn out to be a small price to pay for my peace of mind.
> Every day, let me take a quiet time for reflection and review.

STEP ELEVEN

Sought through prayer and meditation to improve our conscious contact with God as we understood Him, *praying only for knowledge of His will for us and the power to carry that out.*

Can I possibly doubt that prayer and meditation can help me?

Do I pray for things, for advantages, for specific working out of my problems, or simply for the knowledge that the hand of God is guiding me?

Have I discovered that meditation can reveal solutions I hadn't dreamed of, because in meditating I open my mind to inspiration?

Can I ever say that prayer and meditation do not work because they did not produce the results I expected?

Do I realize that "knowledge of God's will" comes to us only with our perfect surrender?

Have I prayed for the alcoholic's sobriety and meditated on the alcoholic's faults, thus keeping my prayer and meditation on a level at which nothing can change for me?

The spiritual exercise suggested by the Eleventh Step is a powerful force for good in our lives. Let me not ever think I have no time for it. I would be depriving myself of precious help.

STEP TWELVE

Having had a spiritual awakening as the result of these steps, we tried to carry this message to others, and to practice these principles in all our affairs.

Do I define a spiritual awakening as the realization of spiritual values within myself?

Does it mean to me the growth of understanding of my own destiny, which I alone can fulfill?

Have I expected this awakening to come to me in the form of instant revelation, and was I disappointed that it did not?

Am I willing to build toward it, watching its gradual growth and profiting from it each day?

Having become aware that I have something to give to others, will I carry this light to those in need?

Do I realize that helping others does even more for me than for them? That "carrying the message" is an obligation I have to myself?

Let me remind myself that in carrying the message, what I do speaks louder than what I say.
Let me not dilute the effectiveness of the help

I can give by letting it take the form of giving advice. I know I will never have enough insight into another's life to tell that person what it is best to do.

A Final Thought

Our search should not be so much for a *solution* to a problem, or a way out of our difficulty, no matter how pressing. The search must be for inspiration, for *insight*, and one cannot know what he will do with an insight until he gets one. Part of the necessary condition is to set aside one's own problems and needs, even the urgent and painful ones, and be prepared to receive and act upon the new insight. It may seem to have little relevance to our problem or need, but it may, indeed, point to the new way in which our effort must be directed while we continue to bear our old burdens.

ROBERT K. GREENLEAF

THE TWELVE TRADITIONS

These guidelines are the means of promoting harmony and growth in Al-Anon groups and in the worldwide fellowship of Al-Anon as a whole. Our group experience suggests that the unity of the Al-Anon Family Groups depends upon our adherence to these Traditions:

1. Our common welfare should come first; personal progress for the greatest number depends upon unity.

2. For our group purpose there is but one authority—a loving God as He may express Himself in our group conscience. Our leaders are but trusted servants—they do not govern.

3. The relatives of alcoholics, when gathered together for mutual aid, may call themselves an Al-Anon Family Group, provided that, as a group, they have no other affiliation. The only requirement for membership is that there be a problem of alcoholism in a relative or friend.

4. Each group should be autonomous, except in matters affecting another group or Al-Anon or AA as a whole.

5. Each Al-Anon Family Group has but one purpose: to help families of alcoholics. We do this by practicing the Twelve Steps of AA *ourselves*, by encouraging and understanding our alcoholic

relatives, and by welcoming and giving comfort to families of alcoholics.

6. Our Family Groups ought never endorse, finance or lend our name to any outside enterprise, lest problems of money, property and prestige divert us from our primary spiritual aim. Although a separate entity, we should always co-operate with Alcoholics Anonymous.

7. Every group ought to be fully self-supporting, declining outside contributions.

8. Al-Anon Twelfth Step work should remain forever non-professional, but our service centers may employ special workers.

9. Our groups, as such, ought never be organized; but we may create service boards or committees directly responsible to those they serve.

10. The Al-Anon Family Groups have no opinion on outside issues; hence our name ought never be drawn into public controversy.

11. Our public relations policy is based on attraction rather than promotion; we need always maintain personal anonymity at the level of press, radio, films, and TV. We need guard with special care the anonymity of all AA members.

12. Anonymity is the spiritual foundation of all our Traditions, ever reminding us to place principles above personalities.

TWELVE CONCEPTS OF SERVICE

The Twelve Steps and Traditions are guides for personal growth and group unity. The Twelve Concepts are guides for service. They show how Twelfth Step work can be done on a broad scale and how members of a World Service Office can relate to each other and to the groups, through a World Service Conference, to spread Al-Anon's message worldwide.

1. The ultimate responsibility and authority for Al-Anon world services belongs to the Al-Anon groups.
2. The Al-Anon Family Groups have delegated complete administrative and operational authority to their Conference and its service arms.
3. The right of decision makes effective leadership possible.
4. Participation is the key to harmony.
5. The rights of appeal and petition protect minorities and insure that they be heard.
6. The Conference acknowledges the primary administrative responsibility of the Trustees.
7. The Trustees have legal rights while the rights of the Conference are traditional.
8. The Board of Trustees delegates full authority for routine management of Al-Anon Headquarters to its executive committees.
9. Good personal leadership at all service levels is a

necessity. In the field of world service the Board of Trustees assumes the primary leadership.

10. Service responsibility is balanced by carefully defined service authority and double-headed management is avoided.

11. The World Service Office is composed of selected committees, executives and staff members.

12. The spiritual foundation for Al-Anon's world services is contained in the General Warranties of the Conference, Article 12 of the Charter.

GENERAL WARRANTIES
OF THE CONFERENCE

In all proceedings the World Service Conference of Al-Anon shall observe the spirit of the Traditions:

1. that only sufficient operating funds, including an ample reserve, be its prudent financial principle;

2. that no Conference member shall be placed in unqualified authority over other members;

3. that all decisions be reached by discussion vote and whenever possible by unanimity;

4. that no Conference action ever be personally punitive or an incitement to public controversy;

5. that though the Conference serves Al-Anon it shall never perform any act of government; and that like the fellowship of Al-Anon Family Groups which it serves, it shall always remain democratic in thought and action.

Index